THE HIDDEN FACE OF TECHNOLOGY

Social Engineering and the Art of Manipulation

Maximiliano Veridian

amazon

CONTENTS

INTRODUCTION TO SOCIAL ENGINEERING

Uncovering Manipulation Tactics

S ocial engineering is a sophisticated manipulation technique aimed at exploiting human nature to gain valuable information or influence people's behavior. It relies on understanding psychological processes, emotions, and human vulnerabilities to deceive and persuade individuals to act in accordance with the manipulator's objectives.

In this chapter, we will delve into the foundations of social engineering and how it is intrinsically linked to the digital age. We will unravel the manipulation tactics employed by social hackers and examine the underlying psychological principles that make this approach effective.

Understanding Social Engineering

Social engineering is an art that has existed since time immemorial but has found new fertile ground in the digital era. It capitalizes on the exploitation of human weaknesses, such as trust, curiosity, and the desire to help, to gain access to privileged information or induce people to take specific actions.

Pillars Of Social Engineering

Several pillars support social engineering, including:

Psychological manipulation: Social hackers leverage people's emotional vulnerabilities, exploiting their needs, fears, and desires. They use persuasive techniques to influence individuals' thoughts and behavior.

Trust engineering: Building trust is essential for the success of social engineering. Manipulators create convincing personas and establish false relationships to gain the trust of victims.

Information exploitation: Information gathering is a crucial part of social engineering. Social hackers investigate their victims, researching publicly available personal information and using it to craft personalized and convincing approaches.

Types Of Social Engineering Attacks

There are different types of social engineering attacks, each with its objectives and specific approaches. Examples include:

Phishing: Phishing involves creating fake emails, messages, or websites posing as trusted entities with the goal of obtaining confidential information such as passwords, credit card numbers, or personal data.

Pretexting: Pretexting involves creating a false story or scenario to obtain information from a person. The manipulator pretends to be a trustworthy person or institution to deceive the victim and gain access to valuable information.

In-Person Social Engineering: This type of attack occurs face-to-face, where social hackers use persuasion and manipulation techniques to gain physical access to a restricted location or sensitive information.

Consequences Of Social Engineering

Social engineering attacks can have devastating consequences for both individuals and organizations. Victims may have their identities stolen, bank accounts compromised, or be manipulated into revealing confidential information. Companies may experience financial losses, damage to their reputation, and the compromise of sensitive data.

The Importance Of Awareness And Education

Awareness and education are fundamental in the fight against social engineering. It is essential for people to understand the tactics used by social hackers and be prepared to identify and protect themselves against potential attacks. Education also plays a crucial role in strengthening cybersecurity and fostering a culture of caution.

In this book, we will explore in detail various social engineering tactics, real case studies, and defense strategies to help readers guard against these threats. As we progress through the following pages, we will dive into the depths of the human mind, unveiling the hidden face of technology and revealing the tactics and secrets of social engineering.

THE POWER OF PERSUASION

Techniques of Psychological Manipulation

Psychological manipulation is a powerful tool in the hands of social engineers who exploit human psychology to influence and persuade people to act according to their desires. In this chapter, we will explore some of the most common techniques used in psychological manipulation, understanding how they work and how we can protect ourselves from them.

Principles Of Persuasion

There are several principles of persuasion often exploited by manipulators. The first of these is reciprocity, which is based on the sense of obligation we feel to repay favors. When someone offers us something, we feel pressured to offer something in return.

Another principle is scarcity, which capitalizes on the fear of losing something valuable. When we perceive that something is in limited quantity or may disappear soon, we tend to value it more and act quickly to obtain it.

Social proof is another powerful principle. We are influenced by the behavior and approval of others. When we see other people acting in a certain way, we tend to follow suit, especially if we consider these people as similar to us or as experts in the field.

Emotional Triggers

Psychological manipulation often uses emotional triggers to influence our decisions. Nostalgia, for example, evokes positive feelings about the past, leading us to make decisions based on those emotions.

Creating anxiety is also a common technique. Manipulators can exploit our fears and insecurities to motivate us to act in line with their interests. For instance, they may create a sense of urgency or imminent threat to pressure us into making hasty decisions.

Language Manipulation

The careful choice of words and phrases also plays a significant role in psychological manipulation. Manipulators can use vague or ambiguous terms to confuse and manipulate our interpretation of information. They may also employ persuasive language techniques, such as repeating key ideas or using emotionally charged language.

Online Persuasion

With the growth of online interactions, psychological manipulation has found a new fertile ground to proliferate. Manipulators can take advantage of anonymity on the internet to create false identities and gain people's trust.

Furthermore, social media and personalized algorithms allow manipulators to target and direct specific messages to influence particular groups of people. They can create echo chambers of opinions and reinforce existing beliefs to manipulate people's behavior and decision-making.

Protecting Against Manipulation

The best defense against psychological manipulation is knowledge and awareness. By understanding the techniques used by manipulators, we can recognize them when applied to us. It's also crucial to cultivate critical thinking and question information, sources, and intentions behind certain messages.

Another form of protection is developing emotional regulation skills. By recognizing our own emotions and vulnerabilities, we can make more conscious decisions and resist manipulative influences.

Psychological manipulation is a powerful tool in the hands of social engineers who exploit human psychology to influence and persuade people to act according to their desires. In this chapter, we have explored some of the most common techniques used in psychological manipulation, understanding how they work and how we can protect ourselves from them.

Principles Of Persuasion

There are various principles of persuasion frequently exploited by manipulators. The first of these is reciprocity, which is based on the sense of obligation we feel to return favors. When someone offers us something, we feel pressure to offer something in return.

Another principle is scarcity, which capitalizes on the fear of losing something valuable. When we perceive that something is in limited quantity or may disappear soon, we tend to value it more and act quickly to obtain it.

Social proof is another powerful principle. We are influenced by the behavior and approval of others. When we see other people acting in a certain way, we tend to follow suit, especially if we perceive these people as similar to us or as experts in the field.

Emotional Triggers

Psychological manipulation often employs emotional triggers to influence our decisions. Nostalgia, for example, evokes positive feelings about the past, leading us to make decisions based on these emotions.

The creation of anxiety is also a common technique. Manipulators can exploit our fears and insecurities to motivate us to act in accordance with their interests. For instance, they may create a sense of urgency or imminent threat to pressure us into making hasty decisions.

Language Manipulation

The careful choice of words and phrases also plays a significant role in psychological manipulation. Manipulators may use vague or ambiguous terms to confuse and manipulate our interpretation of information. They may also employ persuasive language techniques, such as repeating key ideas or using emotionally charged language.

Online Persuasion

With the growth of online interactions, psychological manipulation has found a new fertile ground to proliferate. Manipulators can take advantage of anonymity on the internet to create false identities and gain people's trust.

Furthermore, social media and personalized algorithms allow manipulators to target specific messages to influence certain groups of people. They can create echo chambers of opinions and reinforce existing beliefs to manipulate people's behavior and decision-making.

Protecting Yourself From Manipulation

The best defense against psychological manipulation is knowledge and awareness. By understanding the techniques used by manipulators, we can recognize them when applied towards us. It is also essential to cultivate critical thinking and question information, sources, and intentions behind certain messages.

Another form of protection is developing emotional regulation skills. By recognizing our own emotions and vulnerabilities, we can make more conscious decisions and resist manipulative influences.

SOCIAL HACKER PROFILES

Who Are the Digital Manipulators?

I n the realm of social engineering, social hackers are experts in manipulation and persuasion, skillfully exploiting human nature to achieve their objectives. In this chapter, we will explore who these digital manipulators are by examining their profiles and characteristics. Understanding the identity of social hackers will better prepare us to guard against their deceptive tactics.

Motivations and Psychology: Social hackers may have various motivations for their manipulative actions. Some seek to obtain confidential information, while others aim to cause harm or personal gain. Understanding their motivations provides us with a clearer insight into their intentions and targets. Additionally, we will delve into the psychology behind social hackers, including traits such as empathy, social skills, and behavioral knowledge.

Observation Skills: An essential aspect of social hackers is their keen observational skills. They can identify and analyze subtle information about their targets, such as body language, facial expressions, and tone of voice. These skills enable social hackers to interpret people's reactions and emotions, adapting their manipulation strategies accordingly.

Empathy and Persuasion: Social hackers often master empathy, putting themselves in the shoes of others to understand their needs and desires. They leverage this ability to create emotional connections and establish trust with their victims. Furthermore, we will address the persuasion strategies employed by social hackers, including crafting compelling narratives, exploiting cognitive biases, and using influence techniques.

Technical Knowledge: While social hackers primarily focus on human manipulation skills, many also possess solid technical knowledge. They understand IT systems, security vulnerabilities, and weaknesses in digital defenses. This combination of social and technical skills allows them to exploit security gaps and execute sophisticated attacks.

Social Hacker Profiles: There are different profiles of social hackers, each with its own distinct characteristics. Let's explore some of the most common profiles, such as the "Persuasive Charmer," who uses charisma and social skills to obtain information; the "Technical Social Engineer," who combines technical knowledge with manipulation skills; and the "Emotional Manipulator," who exploits people's emotions to achieve their goals.

DECEIVING THE SENSES

Exploring Perceptual Illusions

I n this chapter, we will delve into the illusions of perception and how digital manipulators exploit our senses to gain an advantage. Through carefully designed techniques, they create illusions that lead us to take specific actions or believe in false information. Let's explore some of the most common tricks used in social engineering and understand how our own senses can deceive us.

The Importance of Perception: Perception is the foundation of our interaction with the world around us. It shapes our understanding of reality and influences our decisions and behaviors. Digital manipulators grasp this importance and leverage vulnerabilities in our perception to gain control over us.

Visual Illusions: Manipulators use visual illusions to deceive us and direct our attention where they want. They exploit the effect known as "selective focus," where our attention is drawn to specific stimuli, while other details go unnoticed. We'll discuss examples of visual illusions, such as the use of colors, contrast, and lighting to create a false impression.

Auditory Illusions: Our ears can also be deceived. Manipulators employ sound manipulation techniques, such as creating ambiguous sounds or overlaying voices, to confuse our auditory perception. We'll discuss examples of auditory illusions and how they can be used to induce specific emotional and behavioral responses.

Tactile Illusions: While tactile manipulation is not as common in the digital context, it is still relevant in certain situations. We'll explore how manipulators can exploit our sense of touch in social engineering strategies, such as manipulating tactile interfaces to induce specific responses or build trust.

Illusions of Time: Digital manipulators often play with our perception of time to prompt hasty decisions or influence our emotions. We'll discuss how creating a sense of urgency, manipulating deadlines, and altering temporal expectations can be used to deceive us.

The Influence of Illusions in Social Engineering: It is crucial to recognize that the influence of illusions in social engineering aims to manipulate our feelings, decisions, and behaviors. By becoming aware of these techniques and adopting a critical stance toward the information we encounter online, we can reduce our susceptibility to manipulation.

Education and awareness are powerful tools to combat the influence of illusions in social engineering. By learning about these techniques and understanding their consequences, we will be better equipped to identify manipulation attempts and protect our data, privacy, and security.

In an increasingly connected and technology-dependent world, it is essential to be vigilant about the methods used by digital manipulators. Understanding perceptual illusions enables us to be more critical, question suspicious information, and make informed decisions, avoiding falling into traps and protecting ourselves from the risks of social engineering.

SOCIAL ENGINEERING ON SOCIAL NETWORKS

Exposing Our Digital Lives

S ocial networks have become an essential part of modern digital life, allowing people to connect, share information, and interact on a global scale. However, these platforms have also become targets for social manipulators and hackers who exploit social engineering to gain unauthorized access to personal information and influence behavior. In this chapter, we will explore the impact of social engineering on social networks and how our digital lives are being exposed.

The Illusion Of Privacy

Many social media users have a false sense of privacy, believing that their information and activities are secure and restricted to a select circle of friends. However, social manipulators are adept at exploiting inappropriate privacy settings and security loopholes on platforms to collect personal information and create detailed profiles of victims.

Social Engineering Through Fake Profiles

A common method of social engineering on social networks is the creation of fake profiles. Social manipulators craft convincing fictional identities and establish connections with potential victims. They may use these profiles to obtain confidential information such as birthdates, phone numbers, and location details.

Phishing And Spear Phishing Attacks

Another common tactic is the use of phishing and spear phishing attacks on social networks. Social manipulators send fraudulent messages posing as friends or acquaintances, requesting personal information, passwords, or even inducing victims to click on malicious links. These techniques exploit the existing trust within social networks to gain unauthorized access to accounts and sensitive data.

Social Engineering And Behavioral Influence

In addition to gathering information, social engineering on social networks seeks to influence behavior. Social manipulators may create disinformation campaigns, spread rumors, or craft manipulative narratives to manipulate public opinion. They exploit our patterns of interaction and content sharing to promote specific agendas.

Protecting Against Social Engineering On Social Networks

To guard against social engineering on social networks, it is essential to adopt proper cybersecurity practices:

Check privacy settings: Review and adjust privacy settings on your social network accounts, limiting access to your personal information.

Be wary of suspicious requests: Exercise caution when receiving friend requests or messages from unknown individuals. Verify the authenticity of profiles before sharing personal information.

Strengthen passwords and authentication: Use strong and unique passwords for each social network account. Consider implementing two-factor authentication for an additional layer of security.

Stay vigilant against disinformation campaigns: Verify the accuracy of information before sharing. Look for reliable sources and research the facts behind stories before believing them.

Educate yourself on social engineering: Be aware of the tactics used by social manipulators and stay updated on the latest scams and attacks.

THE ART OF
DECEPTION

*Advanced Tactics of Digital
Manipulation*

I n the world of social engineering, digital manipulators are true artists of deception. They exploit human nature, employing advanced tactics to influence and persuade their victims. In this chapter, we will explore some of the most sophisticated tactics used by digital manipulators and how they can be applied effectively.

Engagement-Based Social Engineering

Engagement-Based Social Engineering is a sophisticated tactic of digital manipulation that focuses on establishing an emotional connection with the victim to obtain valuable information or influence them in some way. Digital manipulators invest time and effort in building false relationships, taking advantage of the human tendency to seek meaningful connections and interactions.

In this approach, manipulators use various techniques to actively engage the victim. A common strategy is personalized phishing, where they create compelling and customized messages that mimic legitimate communications from trusted companies, organizations, or individuals. These messages can be sent via email, direct messages on social networks, or even phone calls.

Engagement-Based Social Engineering requires detailed research on the victim and the creation of a careful profile. Digital manipulators gather publicly available information, such as social media posts, work histories, personal interests, and connections with other people. Based on this information, they customize their approaches, making them more persuasive and convincing.

Additionally, digital manipulators are skilled at identifying weaknesses and emotional needs of the victims. They exploit vulnerabilities, such as the desire for acceptance, the need for recognition, or the need for a solution to a specific problem. By positioning themselves as someone who can fulfill these needs, they gain the victim's trust and influence them to act as desired.

This approach may also involve the creation of compelling stories or fictional characters that evoke positive emotions in the victim. Digital manipulators may share fictitious personal details, stories of overcoming challenges, or even invented traumas to generate empathy and establish a deeper emotional connection.

Engagement-Based Social Engineering is particularly dangerous because it exploits trust and the human tendency to relate to others. Victims may be led to share personal information, provide passwords, click on malicious links, or even perform unwanted financial actions.

Reciprocity Exploitation

The exploration of reciprocity is a widely employed tactic by digital manipulators in social engineering. This strategy capitalizes on the fact that humans have an innate tendency to reciprocate favors and positive gestures. Digital manipulators leverage this predisposition to gain advantages and influence their victims.

A common example of reciprocity exploitation is when a digital manipulator offers something of apparent value to the victim. It could be a gift, a free sample of a product or service, or anything that sparks interest and elicits a sense of gratitude. Upon receiving something unexpectedly, the victim feels compelled to return the favor, often providing sensitive information or performing actions requested by the manipulator.

Furthermore, digital manipulators may employ the "commitment and consistency" technique. They begin by requesting small, harmless favors or information, creating a sense of commitment in the victim. As the interaction progresses, the requests gradually become more intrusive or demanding. Motivated by the desire to maintain consistency and fulfill previous requests, the victim tends to continue cooperating, even if it compromises their security or privacy.

It is important to note that reciprocity exploitation is not necessarily negative in all situations. In many cases, reciprocity is a healthy part of human interactions and can strengthen relationships. However, digital manipulators use this human tendency to gain personal benefits, often violating the trust of victims and causing significant harm.

To protect against reciprocity exploitation, it is crucial to be aware of the tactics used by digital manipulators. Be wary of gifts or overly generous offers from strangers, especially if they are seeking personal information in return. Maintain a critical stance towards unexpected requests and carefully assess the risks and benefits before sharing information or taking any action.

Pretext And False Authority

In the world of social engineering, the use of pretexts and false authority is a widely employed tactic by digital manipulators. This strategy relies on the ability to disguise oneself as a figure of authority or a trustworthy person to gain access to sensitive information or convince victims to perform certain actions.

Digital manipulators excel at creating plausible pretexts that appear legitimate and convincing. They may pose as representatives of companies, government agencies, financial institutions, or even ordinary individuals to gain the trust of victims. This false persona is crafted to establish a connection and facilitate manipulation.

A common example of this tactic is phishing, where digital manipulators send fake emails or messages that appear to be from a trustworthy source. They may use the company's logo and design, along with persuasive language and persuasion techniques, to convince the victim to disclose confidential information such as passwords, credit card numbers, or personal data.

Additionally, digital manipulators may exploit the trust people have in authority figures, such as high-ranking executives, IT professionals, or even celebrities. They create false identities and use convincing arguments to make victims believe they are dealing with legitimate and trustworthy individuals.

Once the digital manipulator has established a connection with the victim, they can begin to request sensitive information, such as account passwords, banking details, or even persuade the victim to take harmful actions, such as installing malicious software on their device.

Fear And Urgency Exploitation

The exploration of fear and urgency is a powerful and common tactic employed by digital manipulators in social engineering. This approach relies on creating situations of pressure and fear, leading victims to act impulsively without considering the consequences.

Digital manipulators employ a variety of strategies to exploit fear and urgency and achieve their goals. Some examples include:

Security Threats: Manipulators may send false messages warning of a supposed security breach or account invasion. They may claim that the victim needs to provide personal information, such as passwords or credit card numbers, immediately to prevent harm.

Fraudulent Charges: Manipulators may send fake notifications of charges or outstanding debts, asserting that the victim must make immediate payment or face serious consequences, such as legal action or financial restrictions.

Loss of Service Access: Manipulators may state that the victim is at risk of losing access to an important service, such as an email or social media account, if immediate action, such as providing login information or confirming personal data, is not taken.

These tactics exploit people's natural anxiety about their personal security, finances, or access to essential services. Digital manipulators take advantage of the fact that in situations of fear and urgency, people tend to make quick and impulsive decisions without fully evaluating the presented information.

Empathy And Emotional Exploitation

In the context of social engineering, empathy and emotional exploitation are powerful tactics used by digital manipulators to gain the cooperation of victims. These strategies are based on understanding human emotions and the ability to manipulate them to achieve objectives.

Digital manipulators are adept at presenting themselves as allies and demonstrating empathy toward the concerns and needs of victims. They create an emotional connection, establishing trust and sympathy. This connection is crucial for paving the way for subsequent manipulation.

One way to exploit empathy is through sad or touching stories. Digital manipulators can create narratives that appeal to the emotions of victims, evoking compassion and understanding. By sharing personal stories of difficulties, tragedies, or triumphs, they seek to garner empathy from victims, making them more susceptible to their requests.

Emotional exploitation can also involve direct emotional appeals, such as fear, guilt, or gratitude. Digital manipulators may use veiled threats, insinuations of negative consequences, or promises of rewards to influence the emotions of victims. By creating a sense of urgency or making victims feel guilty for not acting, they increase the likelihood of obtaining the desired response.

Emotional manipulation is particularly effective because many people are naturally influenced by emotions. Human decisions and actions are often motivated by feelings and emotional responses, and digital manipulators exploit this vulnerability. They aim to control the emotions of victims, directing them toward a specific behavior or desired response.

Social Engineering In Social Media

Social engineering in social media is a powerful tactic employed by digital manipulators to gather information and influence people through social networking platforms. With the growing popularity of social media, these virtual environments have become fertile ground for manipulation and deceit.

Digital manipulators create fake profiles resembling real individuals, establishing connections with potential victims. They may use attractive photos, invented information, and fictional stories to craft a convincing persona. The intent is to gain people's trust, leading them to share sensitive information or take undesirable actions.

One of the most common strategies in social engineering in social media is to exploit the personal information available on people's profiles. Digital manipulators carefully analyze victims' posts, photos, likes, and interest groups to gain knowledge about their preferences, interests, and social connections. Based on this information, they can tailor their attacks, making them more persuasive and compelling.

Digital manipulators can also employ persuasion and influence tactics to manipulate people's emotions. They may present themselves as potential friends, demonstrate empathy, and create a sense of emotional connection. This can cause victims to lower their guard and share personal information or engage in actions they wouldn't normally take.

Additionally, digital manipulators can leverage the viral nature of social media to spread false information, create controversies, and generate confusion. They may disseminate fake news, rumors, or conspiracy theories with the aim of influencing people's thoughts and behaviors.

Exploration Of Curiosity And The Sense Of Novelty

The exploration of curiosity and the sense of novelty is a powerful tactic used by digital manipulators in social engineering. Humans are naturally curious and have an intrinsic desire to discover new and interesting things. Digital manipulators are aware of this and exploit this characteristic to attract their victims.

One common way to exploit curiosity is through intriguing stories or exclusive information. Digital manipulators create catchy headlines, teasers, or promises of surprising and engaging content to capture people's attention. They arouse individuals' curiosity, making them want to learn more about the subject.

Furthermore, digital manipulators also use the sense of novelty to attract their victims. They present something that appears to be new, innovative, or exclusive, piquing people's interest in experiencing or learning more about this novelty. This can involve products, services, information, or opportunities that seem unique and differentiated.

This tactic is often used in phishing campaigns, where digital manipulators send emails or messages with intriguing content, promising access to privileged information or something extraordinary. By arousing curiosity and the sense of novelty, they manage to make victims click on malicious links, share personal information, or perform undesirable actions.

It is important to note that, when exploring curiosity and the sense of novelty, digital manipulators often use psychological manipulation techniques to create a sense of urgency or scarcity. They may claim that the opportunity is limited in time or available only to a restricted number of people, encouraging victims to act quickly before missing out.

REAL CASES OF SOCIAL ENGINEERING

Studies of Significant Incidents

In the previous chapter, we discussed the tactics and techniques employed by social engineers in social engineering. Now, let's delve into real cases of social engineering incidents that have occurred in the past. These case studies will provide concrete examples of how psychological manipulation was used to gain unauthorized access to sensitive information. By analyzing these incidents, we can better understand the strategies employed by social engineers and learn from the lessons gleaned.

Case Study 1: The Twitter Attack

In July 2021, Twitter became the target of a significant attack resulting in the compromise of several high-profile verified accounts. This incident garnered media and public attention, underscoring the importance of cybersecurity and social engineering as a real threat.

In the Twitter attack, the assailants utilized social engineering as part of a broader strategy to access the platform's internal tools. They posed as Twitter employees, employing persuasive tactics to convince other employees to disclose confidential login information. By gaining access to internal tools, the attackers executed a cryptocurrency fraud scheme, posting deceptive tweets soliciting Bitcoin donations.

A subsequent investigation revealed that the hackers exploited employees' trust and identified weaknesses in Twitter's internal process security. They employed psychological manipulation techniques to persuade employees to share authentication information, such as passwords or access codes.

This case underscores the importance of awareness and cybersecurity training, not only for technical teams but for all employees within an organization. Social engineering relies on psychological manipulation and exploiting individuals' vulnerabilities, such as trust and the desire to help. Therefore, it is crucial for organizations to invest in awareness programs to educate employees about the risks associated with social engineering and how to recognize potential manipulation attempts.

Additionally, the Twitter attack emphasizes the importance of robust security measures, such as two-factor authentication, controlled access to sensitive information, and continuous monitoring of suspicious activities. Safeguarding an organization's data and systems should be a priority, and implementing appropriate security practices is essential to prevent social engineering attacks and minimize damage in the event of incidents.

Case Study 2: The Attack On Equifax Bank

In 2017, Equifax, one of the largest credit reporting agencies in the United States, fell victim to a massive cyberattack that resulted in the exposure of personal data for approximately 147 million individuals. This incident underscored the devastating consequences that a successful social engineering attack can have, not only for the affected organization but also for the individuals whose information was compromised.

The hackers exploited a vulnerability in Equifax's web system, which the company had not addressed with a security update. They gained access to sensitive data, including names, Social Security numbers, dates of birth, addresses, and, in some cases, credit card numbers. The attack was carried out using a technique known as phishing, where hackers send fake electronic messages, appearing to be legitimate, to deceive users and coax them into revealing confidential information.

The investigation revealed that the intruders conducted a targeted phishing attack on an Equifax employee by sending a seemingly legitimate email requesting an update to their access credentials. Deceived by the authentic appearance of the email, the employee inadvertently provided their authentication information, enabling the hackers to access Equifax's internal systems.

The impact of this attack was immense, both for Equifax and the millions of individuals whose information was compromised. In addition to the financial and reputational damage to the company, affected individuals faced the risk of identity theft, financial fraud, and other forms of misuse related to exposed personal data.

Case Study 3: The Dnc Cyber Attack

During the 2016 United States presidential election period, the Democratic National Committee (DNC) fell victim to a sophisticated cyber attack with broad political and national security implications. The attackers aimed to obtain confidential information and undermine the Democratic Party's political campaign.

The DNC attack vividly illustrated how social engineering can be employed as part of a complex cyber strategy. The invaders utilized phishing and spear-phishing techniques to gain access to DNC employees' email accounts. They carefully crafted email messages, appearing legitimate, and targeted specific individuals within the committee.

These persuasive emails were designed to deceive recipients into clicking malicious links or providing their login credentials. By doing so, the attackers successfully gained access to a vast amount of confidential information contained in the compromised email accounts.

The stolen documents and emails were subsequently publicly disclosed, significantly impacting the political landscape and the electoral campaign. The disclosed information had political implications, exposed internal divisions within the party, and influenced public perception of the candidates.

The investigation into the case involved various cybersecurity agencies, including the Federal Bureau of Investigation (FBI) and private company security experts. Although attributing the attack's authorship with certainty proved challenging, many pieces of evidence pointed towards an operation conducted by a foreign government.

Case Study 4: The Attack On The Bangladesh Bank

In 2016, one of the largest cyber attacks related to social engineering occurred at the Bangladesh Central Bank. The hackers aimed to steal approximately $1 billion and successfully executed fraudulent transfers in an impressive manner. This case highlighted the devastating consequences of a successful social engineering attack.

The hackers behind this attack devised a sophisticated plan that began with sending spear-phishing emails to bank employees. These emails were carefully crafted to resemble official internal communications, leading employees to believe they were legitimate. The emails contained malicious attachments or links to fake websites requesting authentication information.

By opening the attachments or providing the requested information on fake websites, bank employees inadvertently allowed hackers to gain access to the bank's internal network. With access to the bank's systems, the intruders could move around and gain control over the funds transfer software.

The hackers exploited a vulnerability in the SWIFT (Society for Worldwide Interbank Financial Telecommunication) system, a global network used by financial institutions for international transfers. They manipulated the bank's funds transfer software to send fraudulent transfer requests to accounts in other countries.

Despite some of the transfer requests being blocked by receiving banks, the hackers still managed to successfully complete transfers totaling tens of millions of dollars. However, the total amount they intended to steal would have been much higher if not for a typographical error in one of the transfer requests, drawing the attention of the involved financial institutions.

Following the attack, a detailed forensic investigation was conducted to determine the causes and those responsible for the incident. It was discovered that the hackers were skilled and possibly linked to a foreign hacker group. The case generated significant international repercussions and raised questions about cybersecurity in the financial sector and the need to strengthen protection measures against social engineering attacks.

SOCIAL AND POLITICAL ENGINEERING

Manipulation in the Spheres of Power

Social engineering extends beyond individual and technological aspects of modern life. It also plays a significant role in political spheres, where manipulation and influence can be wielded to shape opinions, steer agendas, and impact large-scale decisions. In this chapter, we will explore the intersection of social engineering and politics, examining how it is employed in political processes and its implications for society.

Manipulation Of Public Opinion

Social engineering is a powerful tool for manipulating public opinion. Politicians, parties, and interest groups can leverage psychological manipulation techniques to influence people's perceptions and attitudes. From crafting persuasive narratives to strategically disseminating information, these tactics are employed to garner popular support and shape opinions in favor of specific political agendas.

A classic example of public opinion manipulation is political propaganda. Through persuasion techniques such as the use of catchy slogans, impactful imagery, and emotional speeches, politicians can gain followers and influence how people perceive complex political issues. Additionally, the strategic use of social media and digital platforms has expanded the reach of these strategies, allowing political messages to be precisely and selectively targeted.

Corruption And Electoral Manipulation

Social engineering can also manifest in corrupt practices and electoral manipulation. Vote-buying, the spread of misinformation, voter suppression, and other unethical techniques are employed to influence election results and ensure a grip on power. These practices undermine the integrity of democratic processes, compromising the representativeness and will of the people.

Furthermore, social engineering may be present behind the scenes of electoral campaigns, where manipulation strategies are employed to secure donors, obtain illegal funding, and influence election outcomes. This underscores the importance of effective oversight and measures to combat corruption in the political system.

Citizen Responsibility

It is essential for citizens to be aware of the influence of social engineering in politics and be capable of identifying and questioning manipulative strategies. Civic education, awareness of misinformation, and critical analysis skills are crucial tools for resisting political manipulation.

Moreover, transparency and accountability in political processes are fundamental. Control mechanisms, regulations, and a free press are essential to ensure that politicians and interest groups act ethically and responsibly.

SOCIAL ENGINEERING IN INTERPERSONAL RELATIONSHIPS

Influencing People

S ocial engineering goes beyond the digital environment and also manifests in day-to-day interpersonal interactions. In this chapter, we will explore how manipulators use social engineering techniques to influence people, delving into their psychology and exploiting their emotional vulnerabilities. Let's delve into the strategies employed to gain advantages, persuade, and manipulate in personal relationships.

The Art Of Persuasion

Persuasion is a powerful tool in social engineering. We will explore the persuasion techniques used by manipulators, such as the use of emotional triggers, empathy techniques, and persuasive communication. We will discuss how these strategies can be applied in everyday situations, from sales and negotiations to personal relationships.

Exploring Vulnerabilities

Manipulators are adept at identifying people's emotional vulnerabilities and using them to their advantage. We will investigate how they exploit the need for acceptance, fear of rejection, the quest for validation, and other emotional fragilities to exert influence over individuals. We will also discuss ways to identify and protect oneself against these manipulations.

Manipulation And Control

In addition to persuasion, manipulation and control are strategies often employed by manipulators. We will analyze manipulative techniques such as gaslighting, social isolation, emotional blackmail, and psychological games. We will address warning signs and the harmful consequences of this form of manipulation, as well as strategies for dealing with such situations.

Toxic Relationships

Toxic relationships are often driven by social engineering techniques. We will examine common patterns in abusive relationships, signs of a toxic relationship, and how emotional manipulation can undermine a person's self-esteem and autonomy. We will also discuss the importance of self-care, establishing healthy boundaries, and seeking support in harmful relationship situations.

Resisting Manipulation

In this segment, we will provide strategies for resisting

manipulation and developing emotional resilience. We will address the importance of self-awareness, strengthening self-esteem, and having confidence in oneself. We will also discuss the need to establish clear boundaries, practice assertiveness, and seek healthy and balanced relationships.

SOCIAL ENGINEERING AND MALWARE NETWORKS

Advanced Threats

Social engineering is one of the oldest and most effective tactics employed by cybercriminals to compromise systems and steal confidential information. Over the years, social engineering attacks have evolved from simple phishing emails to highly sophisticated and targeted campaigns that combine psychological techniques with advanced malware threats. In this chapter, we will explore advanced social engineering threats, focusing on malware networks, how they operate, and how we can protect ourselves against them.

The Growth Of Social Engineering-Based Threats

Social engineering is the art of manipulating and exploiting psychological aspects of humans to gain unauthorized access to systems, confidential information, or execute malicious actions.

With the advancement of technology and the growth of social media, cybercriminals have found new opportunities to enhance their techniques and make attacks even more convincing. The threat of social engineering combined with the use of malware networks has been a major concern for individuals and organizations.

Malware Networks: Introduction And Functionality

Malware networks are complex structures composed of a wide variety of compromised components and devices. These networks, also known as botnets, are remotely controlled by cybercriminals and may include millions of zombie devices, such as computers, smartphones, and servers, used for malicious purposes like spamming, DDoS attacks, and information theft.

The Connection Between Social Engineering And Malware Networks

Social engineering plays a crucial role in the propagation and operation of malware networks. Attackers use persuasive techniques, such as highly personalized phishing emails, fake messages on social networks, and malicious links in online advertisements, to attract victims and lead them to perform actions that trigger the malware. Once a device is infected, it can be added to the botnet and used to further expand the network.

Advanced Social Engineering Tactics In Malware Networks

Advanced social engineering tactics in malware networks are becoming increasingly elaborate and challenging to detect. Cybercriminals conduct thorough research on their victims, gathering information from social networks and other online sources to create highly personalized and convincing messages. Phishing emails and messages can now contain accurate information about recipients, such as colleagues' names, details of banking transactions, and even personal interests.

Impacts And Damages Caused By Malware Networks

Malware networks have the potential to cause significant harm to both individuals and organizations. Social engineering-based attacks can lead to the theft of sensitive data, such as banking information and login credentials, resulting in financial losses and identity theft. Additionally, botnets can be used to spread additional malware, compromise privacy, and conduct large-scale attacks, affecting the availability of online services.

SOCIAL ENGINEERING IN DIGITAL ADVERTISING

Influencing the Consumer

D igital advertising has become an omnipresent part of our online lives. While navigating the internet, we are constantly exposed to ads aiming to capture our attention and influence our consumer behavior. However, behind these advertising strategies often lies the application of social engineering techniques designed to manipulate our emotions, desires, and purchasing decisions. In this chapter, we will explore how social engineering is employed in digital advertising and discuss some of the tactics used to influence the consumer.

Understanding Social Engineering In Digital Advertising

Social engineering in digital advertising involves manipulating psychological and social elements to steer consumer behavior.

Advertisers seek to create emotional connections with the target audience by exploiting vulnerabilities and latent desires.

Personalization And Ad Targeting

Ad personalization is an effective strategy for influencing the consumer. Through data collection and analysis, advertisers can tailor their ads based on the interests, preferences, and demographic characteristics of each individual, increasing the chances of engagement and conversion.

Exploring Emotional Triggers

Social engineering in digital advertising aims to trigger emotional responses that influence consumer behavior. These triggers may include creating ads that evoke feelings of nostalgia, fear, social belonging, or status aspirations.

Use Of Social Proof And Influencers

Social proof is a powerful strategy in digital advertising. By showcasing testimonials, positive reviews, follower numbers, or social media engagement, advertisers aim to build trust and influence consumers to make purchasing decisions.

Urgency And Scarcity

Creating a sense of urgency and scarcity is another commonly used technique in digital advertising. By highlighting limited-time offers, reduced stock, or exclusive editions, advertisers aim to expedite the consumer's decision-making process.

Gamification And Rewards

Gamification is an innovative approach in digital advertising, incorporating gaming elements to engage and reward consumers. Through challenges, points, levels, and rewards, advertisers can stimulate consumer participation and loyalty.

Transparency And Ethics In Digital Advertising

While social engineering in digital advertising can be an effective strategy, it is essential to consider transparency and ethical issues. Advertisers must be transparent about the collection and use of consumer data, respecting privacy and providing clear information about their advertising practices.

www.ingramcontent.com/pod-product-compliance
Lightning Source LLC
LaVergne TN
LVHW051622050326
832903LV00033B/4627